Our True Song

poems by

Kevin Arnold

Finishing Line Press
Georgetown, Kentucky

Our True Song

ACKNOWLEDGMENTS

Thankful acknowledgment is made to the editors of the following journals,
anthologies, and national websites, in which some of these poems appeared
earlier:

Journals and Anthologies:
Cæsura, 25th Anniversary Issue—"Japanese Graveyard on Kauai"
Dallas Opera News—"Invitation to the Opera"
eNVee—"Carpaccio," as "Seeds"
Foothill Review—"Summer's Last Swim Meet" as "Free, Fly, Back, Breast"
Manzanita Review—"At Jasper Ridge Ranch" as "At Webb Ranch"
Mokhillian Review of Poetry—"Dancing at Halloween"
Mudfish—"Across the Decades"
Remembering—"Aerobatics in a Time of War"
Slippery Elm—"The Chinese Woman's Voice"
The Clock, Desperados, and Jeremy, the first Zapizdat Review—"Everything
Happens at Once," as "Maverick,"

National Website: YourDailyPoem.com—"Invitation to the Opera;"
"Summer's Last Swim Meet" as "Free, Fly, Back, Breast;" "American
Shakespeare;" "Our True Song;" Daylight Savings Time;" "The Colors of
Jasper Ridge"

Publisher: Leah Huete de Maines
Editor: Christen Kincaid
Cover Art: Buchkiste via Pixels
Author Photo: Scotty Arnold
Cover Design: Elizabeth Maines McCleavy

Order online: www.finishinglinepress.com
also available on amazon.com

Author inquiries and mail orders:
Finishing Line Press
PO Box 1626
Georgetown, Kentucky 40324
USA

Contents

The Milkshake Guy

Familiar with my wife's frailness,
he almost lifts her from the car,
seats us in his busy luncheonette,
and asks if we want the usual—milkshakes.

Often chocolate, always with a cherry,
but this day I offer alternatives.
When she hears "strawberry"
she nods and smiles.

He serves us and all too soon helps her
out of her chair. With the milkshake
guy on one side and me on the other,
she bravely hobbles back to the car.

I probably shouldn't call him
the milkshake guy—he's more than that.
He's big, six foot three, two hundred pounds,
with a halting, smiling kindness to him.

How can I thank him for the reprieve
he's granted us: A few minutes away
from the care home down the street,
a few last moments on a date.

You Must Not Think Badly of Me
—for Auguste and Karl Deter

We remember little of Auguste Deter,
who, in her late forties, would drag sheets
across her house and scream for hours
in the middle of the night.

She was the first woman recorded to have
debilitating memory lapses
due to a strange plaque in her brain.

Nor do we share memories of her care-partner,
Her husband Karl, a railway worker who gave up
and sent her, in 1901, to "The Castle of Insanity"
in Frankfort, Germany.

The one we remember is the doctor
she met there, who asked,
"Where are you right now?"
and recorded her reply:
"Here and everywhere, here and now,
you must not think badly of me."

On her death, he examined her brain.
Using a new chemical, he discovered
twisted fibers—nerve tangles.
We remember Alois Alzheimer.

The Move to Memory Care

Carol had said many times,
if she got Alzheimer's, when
it's time, put her out on a farm
like her parents, who both
died of the disease.

The people from the facility and I
had set everything up. As agreed,
I'd told Carol she was going to lunch.
With my daughter Amelia,
I drove an hour from the Bay Area.

On the way down, Carol asked her,
seven times, how she was doing.
In the back seat with her,
Amelia, bless her,
found new answers every time.

Set in the middle of an apple orchard,
The facility was bucolic.
We'd set up her room with a new bed
and TV and family
and horse pictures on the walls.

They'd even put her name on the door,
which confused her. She turned to me.
I told her it would be okay.
Attendants shooed my daughter and me
away, and guided Carol to her lunch.

The Chinese Woman's Voice

I get a few whiffs of foreign sawdust
while I fondle an imitation Ming vase,
nearly-opaque with blue splotches,
hurriedly hand-painted
and a lid that doesn't quite seat
at an import-store surrounded by
mugs stacked over my head
and dangling tables and baskets.

The sweet-pungent smell drags me not to
fifteenth-century China but
some quick-fingered assembly-line painter.
I feel I can see her now
working furiously at her task.
I probably have things she covets:
money and time to spend with my kids
in a discount East-West shop.
She talks to me says
it's okay, it's okay.

Dancing at Halloween

All parts of love are here with us
as we ask one another to dance,
the women so festive in Halloween garb—
one tribal princess, several bats, a slinky disco woman,
and of course plump pumpkins, perky cowgirls.

Filial love abounds as we all smile too much,
chit-chatting about each other's children
and the price of real estate in the valley we overlook.

Erotic love taps our shoulders as the singer croons.
A few men still pose as predators, but most are cautious now,
single at midlife, and the women, comfortable
in their lonely bodies, know what they have to share.

Agape love is here too,
forgiving errant dance steps and premature marriages,
blessing the few souls not dancing now
and even those like me, making outdated movements
on the dance floor with one of the pumpkins.
I want to tell her that my new love, far away tonight,
is here with us too. The music slows and the singer,
portable mike in hand, walks onto the dance floor
and serenades us: it is time to go home.

American Shakespeare

We watch the stars slowly begin their twinkling
at Red Rocks or Aspen or a park in New York City
or a smaller town where perhaps the Rec Committee
has bent a few rules and the oft-broke Arts Commission

found some funds to get the thespians to memorize
those long soliloquies for almost nothing.
Volunteers have parked cars and ushered
people to their seats to keep ticket prices down,

so the house is packed and the meadows blanketed.
Once the players start, the amazing turns of phrase
transfix us as night moves toward total darkness
and the actors seem so close we can touch them.

In the newfound intimacy we swoon at the lovers'
kisses and that their five-century-old bawdy badinage
is still alive today. Many of us still hope-against-hope
for the lovers to make things work until we slowly admit

again what we've known along: they are star-crossed.
Still we smile as the curtain call looms, knowing Shakespeare
will proclaim an elegant order behind tonight's tragedy,
and, when the players bow deeply, we will rise.

The Colors of Jasper Ridge

You can find occasional dabs of red
or bright yellow, often a wildflower.
In August or September, perhaps
a pink Naked Lady, a Belladonna.

And you can search out some blue,
although you won't find a shade
that can compete with the sky.
Which, today, gets darker overhead.

There's brown soil and bark, and
sand by the lake and on the trails,
but no color on the preserve
can compare with the greens.

On far horizons or next to the trail,
evergreens don't seem to change.
In the fall, the green oaks may turn
vivid red surrounded by verdant grass.

Perhaps you'll see a white serviceberry
near a yellowish-green box elder or
blueish-green chaparral backgrounding
a black and orange butterfly on wing.

This Minute

Come near me, notice
the sky over that way,
above the tall evergreen.

Don't you love the colors?
Hints of moisture interrupt
the deep blue of the sky,

blend into just-slightly-lighter
blue where the cloud starts
and then the purest light blue,

growing fully white
and finally, a touch of gray,
and here, near sunset,

oh, that orange at the cloud's
edge, reflecting the autumn
sun, almost gone now.

I'll be ever thankful you shared
this exact minute with me,
our days almost gone now.

Ants

Nature ain't all flora and fauna—it can
be most messy—think of rats with fleas
or the spider who bit me Tuesday night
leaving an angry red spot on my thigh.

And the ants don't stop. Yesterday
they got into the dishwasher—
I closed it and ran it on Quick Rinse,
yet two of them made it through.

Intriguing little devils, ants. First
lone scouts and later commuter lanes
I read they smell with their antennae
and have many ways to communicate.

Ants can kill the Buddhist in you
—Reverence for all living things—
Today they're into the recycling bin.
I grab the vacuum cleaner, fire it up.

Carpaccio

Wine was already spilled on the pink tablecloth,
the two couples' cheeks already flushed,
but she hadn't noticed,
so when her husband split a shrimp cocktail with Bill's wife,
she surprised herself by joining with Bill to split Carpaccio.

The raw beef came laid out like a flower,
deep red petals on bone plate.

Bill spread capers and minced onions wantonly,
and didn't worry about seeds as he squeezed the lemon.

She could feel his hunger as he gathered the beef,
then, his fork still in his left hand,
took a large red chunk into his mouth;
from next to him she felt she could taste
onionpungent and lemonsour and capersalt—
despite herself she could taste them
merging on his tongue with the cool red flesh;

then in front of God and everybody in the nice restaurant,
in front of their shrimp-cocktail-eating spouses,
lifting her fork over the spilled wine,
she followed Bill's brazen lead.

Invitation to the Opera

I can never toss opera invitations.
When one comes, along with the bills, fundraising
letters from my daughter's pricey college,
small magazines that published my work, journals
I keep renewing but seldom find time to read,
and those gold-embossed credit-card offerings to my ex-wife,
it's the opera offers I can't throw away.

It would be so good for the kids if I could get them to go.
Perhaps I can entice them with a familiar name—
La Traviata, Madame Butterfly, Aida, or Carmen.
Or maybe these colorful ads for the newer ones:
The Death of Klinghoffer or *Nixon in China*—

any program that puts the tenors in tails, the
sopranos in satin. Maybe next season, one
Wednesday, Friday, or Saturday, we'll be there
in a plush velvet seat, waiting for the lights to dim.
Imagine us in that heart-stopping quiet
just before the songs echo into the night.

Early Morning, Amherst

Soon after I set foot in
Emily Dickinson's garden
a sleepy guard appears
"I've been watching" she says
"You've been careful but
underneath there are bulbs—"

We make adjustments as I wait
for my daughter to give her command
when she's ready to snap the shutter.

She wants to master the limitations of this
large-format camera her college loaned her.
It loves light and stillness, she says,
capturing motion with the sun low
is the worst use of its gift
but if you jolt the flower
at just the right moment, Dad,
we might capture
a water-droplet in mid-air.

I wait silently
while the garden-guard watches us,
arms folded. Johnna's face
is hidden by a black cloth
over her head and camera.
I say, One false move and we're dead meat
she says "Hush,"
and finally, "Now! Hit it now!"

Aerobatics in Time of War

I had to rise at oh-dark-thirty,
throw on a one-piece bright-orange flight suit,
listen carefully to the flight instructors,
salute almost everyone,

and finally don my aviator
sunglasses and go up alone,
take a nimble aircraft aloft
for the fun stuff, the aerobatics,

where I could do things like a "stall,"
put the nose straight up intentionally until
the wings lost their lift and my two-ton aircraft
would free-fall almost silently, thousands of feet.

I fought my instincts and relaxed in the slow spiral
until I felt some push-back from the stick,
then pulled with all my strength, both hands, and braced
for the 4-G jolt as the wings regained their lift

and I could level out, much closer to earth now,
and notice those puffy cumulonimbus clouds
that formed along the Florida gulf
against the blue water

and could say my secret mantra:
I will not go to Vietnam.
I will not go
to Vietnam.

Monterey Bay with Whales

I'm overlooking Monterey Bay again
the way I do. This time I mimic
the way the Navy taught me to scan
the horizon many years ago. You don't really

scan. You look in one direction, long
enough to focus on only that direction,
before you move your gaze twenty degrees
to the one side or the other, pause, scan

and so forth until you've examined
the entire vista. Today I find a leaning
sailboat off Santa Cruz and a freighter
way out on the horizon, a mere dot.

Toward the end of my scan, surprisingly
close to shore, I spot two or three whales.
It's springtime, so they've come from
Mexico, where they've been breeding,

heading for arctic feeding with their calves.
I probably spot whales or pods of dolphins
on a quarter of my visits to Monterey Bay.
Unlike pods of dolphins, who surface more,

when a whale dives, it'll be minutes before
you see him again. But patience is rewarded.
This time, the whale spouts. God is in
His heaven and all's right with the world.

A Wave Starts as a Swell

Or the start of a swell,
or the start of a start of a swell,
then grows as our love did, until—
well what a wave does is confront
the remains of prior waves
planes over leftovers until it suddenly crashes,
sometimes with a deadening thunder,
that moment painters paint.

Waves don't die but continue diminished,
duck under earlier waves until they
lap up on a rocky shore or a beach,
finally settle under new waves,
join a powerful undertow
—remember how we'd warn the kids?

First Wife

That summer before we separated
I talked her into tennis lessons—
forehands, backhands, volleys.

I would compliment her strokes
and call lines in her favor,
the kindest opponent in the world.

Afterward I hit balls to her, gentle, soft
shots that lured her slowly to the net, when
with sudden firmness, I hit the ball past her.

Divorce Albums

Next to the wedding books, they
hold a packet for lingerie from secret dates,
with disintegration chapters
for Christmas cards not sent,
children's lunches un-prepared.
A place for the counselers' and lawyers' bills
real-estate commission statements
and photographs of the couple in various stages
of exhaustion, longing, even hate. An entire section
is set aside for the day the kids are told
the two who brought them forth are irreconcilable.

Leather-bound, gold-stamped books are provided
for those who reconcile, wide publicity for
the smiling faces of those who beat the odds.
And the others always have their
wedding and divorce books side by side.
The wedding may have been for the parents
the other is theirs alone.

Longing

Stop me if you've
heard enough longing,

watched me shiver,
wanting wild rivers.

I know you're downstream,
strong enough to pull me out.

God I miss you
on this safe shore.

Heart Grown Up

"It is better for the heart to break,
than not to break."
                    —*Mary Oliver*

Until she broke you, I wasn't sure you
existed. At most, I thought of you
as just another organ—a gall bladder,

a spleen, or a liver. She ensured I felt
heartache not as tired metaphor but
as physical pain. She let you show me joy,

but also watched you radiating agony.
Ahead of me as usual, she introduced
me to my grown-up broken heart.

Japanese Graveyard on Kauai

One afternoon I drove my daughter way past Kappa,
deep into desolate cane-hauling roads.
We came upon an old graveyard on a hill near the ocean.
Before the tall cane it had overlooked the Pacific.

I got out, trying to convey my wonder to my young daughter.
The wooden markers, in Japanese with a little English,
marked the lives of turn-of-the-century fishing families.
I coaxed her out of the car and we walked

to one grave, then another.
One had fresh flowers, but most were overgrown.
I told her about once-prosperous fishing fleets,
gone now. She stood silent.

This is all that's left,
I told her at one family's grave,
after the tortuous trip from Japan,
after building the fishing fleet,

after extracting an honest living from the sea,
after constructing villages—
they're tourist towns today, I said.
No words from her as we returned to the car.

I said I hoped we had more left than that
even though I'd moved away from her mother
and watched her so silent, next to me
in the rental car dwarfed by the sugar cane.

I kept looking over at my small passenger who
wore a cotton skirt over her bathing suit,
peeking up at her father out at the edge of somewhere.
Her eyes said what can he teach me but chaos?

Summer's Last Swim Meet

The six-and-unders sit in numbered chairs,
then hold hands in a daisy-chain
to walk to the proper lane with their team's coach
and stand nervously until the horn sounds,
when they get to splash in and make arm-windmills.
I, the false-start judge, see it all—
their legs that don't contribute much,
and the way they brush the lane-markers
and breathe too often so it seems to take forever.
Still they all finish and how they beam as they climb out!
…As the seven-eights take their places at the start
and at the horn dive straighter out,
stroke with more authority.

My Scotty-boy, normally no star, cuts five seconds off his best time.
And they don't breathe—coach says, after today
you'll have all fall to breathe.
The nine-tens don't hold hands but walk out knowing
this is the combined meet—all the teams are here.
Sure-footed Kate slips in her starting dive and never recovers,
trying to keep up with the eleven-twelves, who really clip along.
But it's the thirteen-and-overs who take your breath away.
They seem to cover the pool in five strokes,
their parents who've shuttled them for years
beaming over this transition from summer to fall,
childhood to adulthood—
this communal concentration on a good start.

Across the Decades

I'm in a theater bar on a rainy evening in Manhattan
with my son, a composer who lives nearby. We sit
in a booth discussing whether or not passion must drive
the arc of a story, how plays and novels might demand
a through story. When he gets up, guys move toward him.

Although he doesn't drink much liquor, he's obviously
among friends here. I stop following his lanky frame,
sip my Merlot and eat a breadstick. When I look up
I see him signaling to the guys to cool it. He's not
looking my way, but I can see him motion toward me.

The people coming from outside enter drenched.
We seldom have such violent rain in California.
It's been ten years since he came out to me, and
decades since I asked his nursery school teachers
if he might already be in a club I could never join.

Norfolk Island Pine

If you study the pine in my front yard, you'll see
it must have gotten almost no sunlight early on.
Its scrawny early branches were stubby,
misshapen with only slights hint of green,

but somehow this tree made it through those
early years, still pitiful at four feet, then six
feet, where it seems to have caught some sun.
At seven feet, finally, the branches start to look

the way a Norfolk Island Pine is supposed
to look. The taller branches are fuller
yet, but if it weren't for those perfectly
shaped top deep green branches that

reach eagerly for the sky, that seem to look
exactly the way a Norfolk Island Pine was
supposed to, I never would have seen myself
in the tree. A strong finish after a tough start.

If you were adequately nurtured as a child,
if your mother wasn't addicted to pills and your
dad could hold a job, you probably just see
a tree with a heartier shade of green on top

than one would expect. I'm most thankful
to those teachers who taught me to stand up
straight. Sometimes they even lifted me on
their shoulders to help me find my own sun.

My Parents Before Me

A photograph of them
courting in Charleston,
the Dartmouth man
sent south by GE,
a dark suit with
a touch of handkerchief.

Her gloves held in her left hand,
she looks unfettered, far from
her mother on the farm
downing pills by the handful.

Her curvehugging beads
caught in mid-sway
give no hint she will follow
in her mother's footsteps
her care will become his life—
just this snappy couple
stepping out.

Everything Happens at Once

I will never forget the moment I first believed
I was born in God, part of a plan so intricate
no mortal could possibly understand it.
That Friday I forgave Billy for
tripping me in the bushes and kicking me—
all was forgiven that day. I was on the path,
and with each breath I let God

       —Hold me—

The way I'd held that stuffed animal, that limp lamb
I clung to after my dog Maverick had been hit by a car.
After Maverick died, his head on my knee, I held the lamb
and started yelling at my mother—Why couldn't she have
been there and told Billy I'd been sick, that I'd been
in a coma, near death? Yet that Friday I knew

      —No one ever dies—

God would forgive me for yelling at my mother.
And I knew, after Billy was punished, he'd be forgiven too.
Forgiveness would be like air.
Maverick was in heaven or on his way.
All things happen at once,
and the joy I found as a child
is still part of me
(though it can fade so easily now)
but I know joy should be now,
can be for ever and forever and ever.

The Soothing Touch of a Currycomb

Cats, horses and dogs know us in
many ways. When we address them
by name, they sometimes seem startled
at our voice, or even thrilled.

They know other words too, stay
and stop and come, and horses know
the secret language of tongue-clucks.
They know who feeds them and

bathes them, and who gives them a
treat, another word they know.
I've never known an animal who
doesn't like to be gently scratched

behind the ears or rubbed down.
Or patiently groomed with
A hard-bristled currycomb.
What they know about us for certain,
they know through touch.

Feeding Other People's Horses

Even after ten years, Snowball, the male
pony, and Crystal, the thirty-year-old
thoroughbred, approach me, stamp a foot
and whinny in anticipation of carrots

and cookies. Of course I pet them. They're
all that's left of my horseback-riding days.
They mean so much, giving me my daily dose
of horse therapy, every day, thirty-five

hundred days of the eight-minute ride to
the hills to see them, not four or five days
a week—every day. When I take vacation,
I provide treats for volunteers who fill in.

People question whether I visit the horses
even when it rains and I ask back, Do you
think the rainy days are easy on them?
There's a small roof that tries to shelter

them, but some days the wind drives the rain
sideways. They shiver in their wet coats.
Those are not the days for me to skip feeding
and touching them, making me feel loved.

The Propeller of Everything

In my dream my son had met this girl, I saw them touching,
so I had to tell him everything at once:
the times you do it when you shouldn't,
the times you don't do it when you should;
the shame when you show desire only to have her tell you,
in no uncertain terms, that you are acting inappropriately,
the *hard-walled loneliness* of that;
the times when sex and love lay upon one another
not just as concentric circles but as the same circle exactly,
the times they aren't even in the same room together,
can't even shout through walls at one another,
yet sex still shouts;

how sex shadows every human interaction,
even between a child like himself and his teachers,
his mother, even his father, me; the way
sex has colored his thinking as long as he can remember,
how sex separated his mother from me,
how it's brought him to wear his bathing suit in the bathtub;
the way the women know they have it to give, or is that wrong,
do we just keep imploring them, or is all that changing;
the way those questions rattle around in the houses of our beings;
how if you include same-sex love there is no end to it,
sex propels everything; even my solitary blind mother,
his grandmother in the nursing home, is shaped by it;
the road he is about to start down has no exit—
but I wake up then, realize my son is only eleven,
I won't say these things to him now, nor probably ever—
to say things like this in real life it is always too early or too late.

The Art Opening

Our daughter Johnna has won three photography awards,
so my ex-wife and I treat her and her artist-friends
to a restaurant dinner after an opening in San Francisco.
We sit one person apart, my ex-wife's husband
on the other side of her, subdued in a tie and tweed jacket.
Johnna sits between us, with little conversation bits filled
with double meanings flit around her, like
despite our differences we have done one thing well,

and my hurt foot, my bruised heel/fallen arch doesn't bother at all.
Johnna, often shy, seems oblivious to her aging mother and father
tonight, she is radiant in her moment, she has survived,
two of the show's sponsors will buy her oversized
black-and-white triptychs, so unexpectedly bold,
for more money than she spends in a month.
I bask in her reflected glory until, just as dessert arrives,
we're reminded the parking lot is closing, so I have to
ransom the car, and I can't get my loafers back on.

Why did I wear new shoes with this foot?
Johnna, suddenly solicitous, walks with me, supporting my arm.
The cold San Francisco winds have come, and every step hurts.
My ex- and her husband in his tweeds walk smoothly ahead.
I hobble and realize I am celebrating my daughter's success before
mine ever happened. I picture an airport, me gunning my plane—
there's not enough runway for me to get airborne. I shiver in my
shirtsleeves as I lean almost all my weight on Johnna now.

Chuck Close in New Haven

Chuck Close has two self-portraits,
one, black ink on white paper, the
other white on black, both use

identical-sized pixels, about one quarter
inch squares, so that there's a logical
reciprocity, where thirty percent gray tone

translates into seventy percent white ink on
black paper at sixteen squares per inch.
But I know Chuck from other museums—

he's a favorite of mine, but he is
always trying to hide in plain sight.
"Come forth, show us who you are,

Chuck, don't play with all that clever
pixilation—come out of the darkness.
All these are representations of you,

Charles Thomas Close, born in Monroe,
Washington, graduate of Yale,
undergrad and grad. Just be Chuck."

Plein Air Plaint

He so loved the natural world that he
joined others who had come to art late
in life to patiently paint nature *al fresco*.

When his wife started having memory
problems, he tried to take it in stride.
She would be fine while he painted.

But things progressed and he spent more
time on doctor's visits and panic attacks,
pills and paperwork; every aspect of her life.

For the last years of her life,
the plein air artist stayed inside with her.
When he rejoined his friends in the open air,

he tried to explain how he'd lived for the
few moments she seemed her old self,
and how she left him before she left him.

First, Do No Harm

No matter how you work
to avoid it, there's no way
around a critical opening.

Even if you have little
confidence you'll finish
successfully, you must make

that first incision. Start
forcefully with the sharpest
instrument in your kitbag.

It's the same for a tumor
on the brain or a deep ache
in the reader's heart.

Poetry and surgery
are ancient brothers
like Romulus and Remus.

Minimize any bleeding
as you excise whatever
you know doesn't belong.

Once mended, close things up
with uniform cross-stitches
X X X X X X X X X X.

If you've operated with your
full attention and decisive care,
that last line begins the healing.

Poet Snow

The artists give us light
how it bends around corners
and all the variations of color.

Musicians give us sounds—
the whirr of a hummingbird's wing
the drumbeat of a needy child.

Writers give us weather—
how hot it got in Atlanta
during the War Between the States.

Graceful poets' verses fall gently
to earth and blanket mountains,
valleys and cities equally, like snow.

Invitation

Sometimes I'm lost in gnarly oaks
but tonight I find myself wandering
amidst hundreds of ruler-straight
redwood trees. I'm in my fantasy world
complete with unicorns and pegacorns
and amiable women without agendas
in California's wildflower-laden rolling hills.

I find an old growth redwood that has died
perhaps felled, now surrounded by a ten-foot
circle of young trees often called a Fairy Circle
or a Cathedral. I build a bed of fronds at its
center, and throw down a blanket. Lying on
my back, I gaze up to the stars, and think
how perfect this would be with a lover.

One of a Handful

Perhaps one love is like another when it ends:
    only the one who wanted it to last
    understands what was at stake.

At least once you must have lived in that lovesick daze
    and glanced up to see someone who looked
    almost exactly like the lover who had scorned you,

and didn't you jump up from your table just to make sure,
    and run full-tilt wherever that person took you,
    driven by adrenaline, driven by hope?

And when, panting, you overtook this stranger,
    what did you do then? Were you apologetic,
    did you say, "Sorry, I mistook you..."

Or did you find the righteous power of the jilted lover
    and set things straight right then and there,
    describing the monstrous treatment you'd received,

you, who could have made it all work! Did you seize the moment
    and tell the tale in that wonderful, out-of-control,
    desperate way that we only get to perform a few times

in real life, standing squarely at center stage for once,
    stating, of all the people on this planet,
    you are one of the handful driven by love?

Our True Song

Our simple acts may be the warp and weft
of the substance of our lives, what is left

beyond the gifts and wills, the trusts and estates
after our *belles lettres* or *plein air* landscapes

what if our day-to-day relationships, in the long
slog of life, form our lasting legacy, our true song?

Milton Keynes UK
Ingram Content Group UK Ltd.
UKHW012150270324
440282UK00003B/16

9 798888 385210